S0-BRS-846

is
that
your
SISTER?

A true story of adoption

BY Catherine and Sherry Bunin

PANTHEON BOOKS

DESIGNED BY SALLIE BALDWIN

Manufactured in the United States of America
10 9 8 7 6 5 4 3 2

Library of Congress Cataloging in Publication Data
Bunin, Sherry.   Is that your sister?
SUMMARY: An adopted six-year-old girl tells about adoption and how she and her adopted sister feel about it.   1. Children, Adopted—United States—Juvenile literature. 2. Brothers and sisters—Juvenile literature. [1. Adoption. 2. Brothers and sisters] I. Bunin, Catherine, joint author. II. Title.
HV875.B86   362.7'34   76-60   ISBN 0-394-83230-2
ISBN 0-394-93230-7 lib. bdg.

For our family and
our special friend
Patty smith

My name is Catherine. I am six years old.
And I am adopted.

I have a sister who is four years old and she is adopted, too. Kids at school or in the park are always asking me, "Is that your *sister?*"

Sometimes when they see my mother, the kids ask, "Is that your *mother?*" I know why they ask me the questions, because my sister and my mother and I don't look anything alike. We don't have the same kind of skin or face or hair. I tell the kids that my sister and I are adopted. Then they ask me, "What's adopted?"

It makes me feel good to know something the other kids don't know about. My friend Melissa knows because she is adopted, too. I don't think she has to explain all the time the way I do because she has blond hair just like her mother has. They look a lot alike.

I try to tell the kids everything I know about adoption, but the more things I try to explain to them, the more things I think of to ask my mother. Like I'll say to some kids, "Well, it's like this. A woman born me, see, but she couldn't keep me and my mommy and daddy wanted me, so they adopted me."

After I tell them that, I ask my mommy, "*Why* couldn't that woman who born me keep me? Didn't she like me?"

My mommy says, "You were just born. She didn't have time to know you and love you. You were very little when she decided to allow your adoption."

Sometimes I want to hear more than just that, and I say, "But why did she *allow* my adoption?" Well, my mommy tries not to lie to me so I'm not surprised when she says, "I don't know. I don't know enough about the woman to know what went on in her mind." Then Mommy will say, "What do *you* think?"

One time I said, "She was a nice lady who was very, very poor. She had no money for food and she wore a sweater with big holes." Another time I said she was young with long hair she wore in a ponytail. I wear a ponytail sometimes. Sometimes I get sad and all mixed up thinking about her. One time I said, "She taught school like Mrs. Freeman and she really loved kids and had guinea pigs in the room. She allowed my adoption because I was too noisy."

We can talk like that for a long time until Mommy says, "It's nice to daydream, but I do know that the woman was an ordinary human

being, not rich or poor, who knew she couldn't go about the serious business of taking care of a child. Not every woman who bears a child can do it, for one reason or another. We can only guess at what her reason may have been."

That's what I end up telling kids about the woman who born me. I say, "Well, she just couldn't cope, I guess."

When we get that out of the way, kids want to know where my mommy and daddy found me. I think they believe those stories about babies being left in baskets on people's doorsteps and about lost little kids being taken in by some good people who give them good food to eat. I don't think things like that really happen. I tell them that most kids get adopted from an adoption agency.

I was too little to remember my adoption agency, but I went to see the agency where my sister Carla came from. It was a nice building with offices and typewriters and a water tank with paper cups on the side that anyone could take if they were thirsty. It looked a little like my daddy's office, but here they take care of the business of kids. We didn't see any kids because kids don't live at the agency. Sometimes they come to visit the way Carla and I did, but kids who haven't been adopted live in foster homes or in other places somewhere.

"What's a foster home?" some kid is sure to ask me. And I tell them that a foster home is a home with a family who takes care of kids until they have a family of their own. Some kids have to stay a long, long time. I didn't. I don't remember my foster family because I was only three months old when I was adopted. My mommy met my foster mother and she liked her because she took such good care of me, but I know from listening to my mommy that some kids aren't so lucky. They get tired of waiting for a family to come along. Even if they like the foster people, kids want their own family, a forever family.

My sister Carla remembers her foster
family very well. She was just about three years
old when she came to live with us. In fact, she
thinks her foster mother was the woman who
born her, but that's not true. I'll explain it to her
better when she gets bigger.

After all the talking and explaining I do
about adoption, kids still don't get it. I know
because someone will always say, "Yeah, but
don't you know who your *real* mom and dad
are?" *I* know, but *they* don't get it. I tell them
that my *real* mom and dad are the mom and dad
who take care of me and love me. They hug me
a lot. They know when my feelings get hurt and
my feelings get hurt a lot. I think loving kids
is what real parents do. All the kids I know
with real parents get treated like that. But no
matter how I try, I can't seem to explain that
very well. I don't know why.

You know, sometimes I hate talking about adoption with a lot of dumb kids and grownups, too. Most grownups don't know any more about adoption than kids and they ask me the same dumb questions. They ask too many questions and it makes me feel funny. It makes me wish my mommy *had* born me and that I looked just like her. I wish when we walked down the street everyone would say we looked alike—like Melissa and her mother. When I tell Mommy this, she says, "That's a beautiful thing to say because that means you love me." I like it when she says that. I like it better than her long answers. Her long answers explain how when I grow up I'll learn to make use of everything about me that is me and I'll be "a beautiful human being." She thinks I'm going to be the first woman President of the United States or someone even better. She can get all excited thinking about me grown-up.

Most of the time I'm glad I was adopted, even if I do have to explain a lot.

My mommy and daddy already had two kids when they adopted me. They could have had more kids, I know, but they knew that there were plenty of kids like Carla and me who wanted a family and they wanted more kids, so it seemed like a good idea for all of us to get together. That's why they went to the adoption agency.

Do you know what the person who works at the agency to bring families together is called? None of the kids ever know that. I do. A social worker. I don't remember my social worker at *my* agency, but I met Carla's social worker lots of times. She visits us and because we like her, she's invited for dinner, too.

When she first came to our house, she
talked to us kids in the family. She asked us if
we'd like to have another kid around. My
brother Nicholas was rotten. He said, "Don't
bring us another one like that," and he pointed
to me. "Why?" asked the social worker. He
said, "She talks too much." That wasn't nice.

I told the social worker I wanted a sister
because there were two boys in the family and
there should be two girls, not just one, me. Now
that was nice. I showed the social worker where
my sister would sleep. In my room, in a
double-decker bed. She'd sleep in the down bunk
and I'd sleep in the up bunk. It was a nice visit,
but Mommy bit her fingernails the whole time.
She worries a lot and she worried about what the
social worker would think about us. She told
Daddy that night that I told the social worker
she was missing a button off her dress. Well, she
was.

The next visit was the best. Two social workers came and they brought Carla for her first visit. One of the social workers was named Martha and she had a purple coat with a hat to match that her mother knitted for her. Both of them had long hair. Carla was real little, with skinny legs. She looked like a doll. Mommy and Daddy had already met her and they were right—all us kids liked her right away.

They came again in a couple of days and this time they brought Carla along to stay with us for good. They brought her clothes and a couple of old toys, and you know what else? Her baby blanket. That little kid loved to hold that blanket and put her finger in her mouth. Me and my brothers made her laugh when we put our fingers in our mouths to show her how she looked.

When Carla first came, she couldn't talk, but now she talks more than I do. I don't know why Nicholas isn't mad at the social worker for

bringing a kid who talks more than I do, but he
isn't. He plays with Carla a lot. I think he plays
with her too much. When I get mad about it, I
go to my bigger brother Alexander and he gives
me chewing gum and some of his iced tea.

After Carla came to stay, the social worker
with the purple coat made a couple more visits
to see how the family was doing. And then
Mommy and Daddy and the social worker—that
was Martha—began talking about going to
court. At first I thought that meant a court
with a judge and a jury and good and bad
lawyers and things like that. I was scared a
bad lawyer might take Carla away. Mommy
explained that no kids are adopted until they
have lived with a family for six months. Then
the family goes before a judge and swears
they want that kid to stay in the family
forever.

I try and try to remember when I went to court. Mommy says it wasn't a court at all. I sat in the judge's office while she and Daddy raised their hands and swore they'd take good care of me. Then I was made lawfully their daughter. Afterwards, we had a big celebration. I sure wish I could remember.

We went to court with Carla in the morning and we were almost late because we couldn't find a taxi big enough to take all of us. See, there were six of us, and Alexander's friend Rickey wanted to come, so there were seven. Finally we got a nice taxi driver who let us sit on each other's laps. When we got to Family Court (that's the name of the place) we met three more people—the two social workers and a lawyer—and that made *ten* of us. The social workers didn't have to come. They came because they wanted to, but the lawyer had to come because she had all the papers Mommy and Daddy had to sign.

Well, a big man came out into the hall and told us to follow him and he took us into an office with a desk and couch and a few chairs. Behind the desk sat a woman judge. She shook everybody's hand, even Rickey's, and she seemed glad to see us. There wasn't enough room for all of us to sit down, so the social workers and Rickey stood up behind the couch that Mommy and Daddy and Carla and I were sitting on. The big man was there, too, and every time the judge wanted to know if that was Mommy's and Daddy's name on a piece of paper, the big man handed it to them and they said, "Yes." There sure were a lot of papers. My mommy looked like she was crying and so did the social workers, but I just wanted the judge to hurry and get it all over with. Carla's shoes were all over my dress because she was moving around so much. That judge took her time though. I guess she wanted to make sure we all knew what we were getting into and that Carla would be in our family forever and ever.

When we left we went right to a restaurant and had another big celebration lunch and we all got to order anything we wanted, which meant millions of French fries.

When I think about it now, it was really nice.

Now that is all I know about adoption. I don't think about it much unless someone starts asking me questions. I don't think Carla thinks much about it either. Neither do Nicholas or Alexander. We are The Family. We fight a lot just like all the families I know. We fight about television and who gets the most cookies and Nicholas gets mad when Carla breaks up his fort and Alexander gets mad at me if I mess up his coin collection.

Mommy yells at all of us and sometimes Daddy brings us ice cream sandwiches when he does the shopping on Saturday.

We don't have much time to think about this adoption business. But when we ride the subway or bus, people stare at us. And when we go to restaurants people look at us too. They look at us nicely. I don't care if they look. I really like it.

And that's all there is to it.

You know what makes me laugh sometimes when I tell my story? Kids. Some of them will always say they wish someone could adopt them. Some of the kids say they think they really *are* adopted, but their parents won't tell them. Those kids probably aren't adopted at all. My mom and dad say parents should be honest with their kids and it wouldn't be honest if they didn't tell them.

So that's my story of adoption.

And here are our pictures ⟶

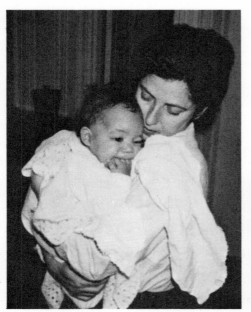

I can't believe
I was ever
this little.

Here's
Daddy

with a beard.

LOOK AT
ALEXANDER
AND NICHOLAS
ALL BUNDLED UP
AND ME TOO.

HERE
WE ARE
iN
MAINE.

I remember
that dress.
Mommy bought it
at a fair.

Watch out!
Here I come!

Mommy
uses this tub
to
wash
the
clothes

when we're in Maine.

Marth
gave u
this
pictur
of
tiny
Carla.

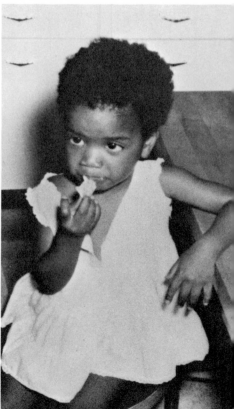

CARLA was
a little scared of us
when she first came.

See how strong
Alexander is!

THESE ARE MY FAVORITE
PICTURES OF EVERYBODY
IN THE FAMILY.

LOOK At CARLA

SMILING!

Catherine Bunin lives in New York City with her mother and father, her sister, Carla, and her two brothers, Alexander and Nicholas. She goes to P.S. 75 and every summer spends a month in Maine, where she would like to live all year round.

Sherry Bunin is Catherine's mother. She is on the staff of the New York Council on Adoptable Children, a citizen's group that she and other adoptive parents organized to help parents adopt children more easily and to help children find their way to a permanent home and a family of their own.